CLOSED FOR REPAIRS

RECOVERY IS A PROCESS...PROCEED WITH CAUTION

BUTT NAKED HONESTY

by Charles Fowlkes

"I left Detroit on February 19, 2006, on a mission to get my life back. I touched down in Madison, WI, on February 20, 2006, sometime in the afternoon. The following is the "genesis" of my embrace with the "Reality of a Made-Up Mind and Commitment to Excellence.""

Dedication

In Loving Memory of my father, Martin; my mother, Estella; my mother-in-law, Sarah; my wife, Nita; my oldest sister, Katherine; my oldest brother, Martin; my brother Billie, my sister Vern, my brother-in-law, C.J.; and my niece, the lovely Michelle.

To my sisters Janet and Vern; they were most supportive and encouraging during my tour of the madness of addiction. I love them both with all my heart!

To all my Family, the Love is Constant, the Love is Sure.

To my Queen—her name is Jennifer. I can hear her telling me, "Just do the damn do, my Husband!"

Mother Earth!

Dedication Continued: My Extended Family

Mashona—we call her "Rae-Rae"—she's straight-up beautiful! She's a little laid back, keeps to herself, but, let me tell you, her laughter is contagious for real! Her wisdom is not displayed upon request, but, trust, me she can hold her own!

Marlon—I call him "Marlino." A very loving individual, and his work ethic is top shelf!

Summer— "Absolutely Gorgeous"—easy to talk to, down to earth, and just like her mama, without a doubt!

Larry, better known as "Cleve." A very talented individual, and in particular areas of life his insight is sharp!

Charles—I call him "C-Smooth." He's the baby of the family but extremely mature; that's my "Young Lion" for real! His intelligence is vibrant and illuminating, a truly awesome fella.

This picture says it all, for sho'!

Closed for Repairs:
"Butt-Naked Honesty"

Table of Contents

Introduction: Word to the Reader: "In the Language of the Street...a Poetical Style"

Allow me to take you on a ride, as I push the rewind button on the tape of my life that will uncover the "root causes," the unfolding of this crazy drama that could have led to my demise (but, fortunately, I'm still here to kick it about)—a lifestyle that had me out there like a broke-down fangless vampire!

My request to the wonderful person reading this manuscript right now is to take out an hour or so of your time and check this out for real! This is not an exhaustive bio of my life, but I have to drop some "Pockets of My History" on you so you can better understand my struggle as well as my eventful comeback! My history reveals devastating memories and troublesome flashbacks, like when I was peeping in the window while my children were having dinner (my crack-head ass wasn't invited). I participated in a few "fantasies"— that this was all just a terrible nightmare, and I would soon wake up—no such luck. Do you feel what I'm saying? (I never could pull off that "fake it 'til you make it," no way)

Many years passed, like 15-20 winters in the "madness of addiction" (crack cocaine, drunkenness, criminal behavior— I was all out of pocket for real!)

When I finally settled my ass down, I was introduced to the process of "Cognitive Restructuring," the invaluable assistance in learning how to overcome destructive thinking and behavior; taking Cognitive Behavioral Therapy to a whole different level. It was time to "listen and participate in some deep-down honest reflection." I gotta keep it real with you: my true intention is to arouse your thinking about this "restructuring process." I'll drop the meaning coming up shortly, but for now I'm gonna keep on giving it to you with this conversational dialogue, seasoned with an appropriate level of professionalism, but I had to "gift wrap it in the language of the street," so you can truly understand how serious this is for real! By the way, there's a noticeable flow of poetic phraseology that will no doubt catch your eye. It was not intentional, but the flow was to my liking, so I left it alone. Are you ready for the ride? Let's go!

The Madness of Addiction

We all have various "addictions" (playing video games, listening to music, reading books, never putting down that phone, etc.).

I'm talking about the "madness of addiction," the excessive, destructive indulgence in a substance or activity or a combination of both: Activities like

- extreme overindulgence in video games or that phone attached to your "unawareness" while you're walking down the street straight up into traffic;
- the pain, fear, and secrecy of childhood trauma;
- the so-called happily married man/woman pursuing sexual encounters one after another, with no regard to what's being brought back into the home;
- criminal behavior;
- being caught up in an unhealthy abusive relationship.

The list is endless.

Many of us were enslaved in an "organized stuck-on-stupid way of living," thoroughly engaged with a Ph.D. in foolishness, just all kinds of nonsense.

Check it out: the acceptance of brutal beatings, the emotional, mental turmoil of losing parental care of your children because you couldn't stay out of the dope house.

Some of us were on a collision course with life in the penitentiary or death. This reality showed up in full force, as many of our family members and friends experienced long periods of incarceration, and a whole lot of us died caught up in the madness.

Some were ashamed or scared to come out in the light of day because their presentation was all out of order. Hiding from the dope man/woman, or not wanting our children to see us like this, we embraced the darkness of night in hot pursuit of drugs, sex, money, isolation, etc.

Others were on "full public display," engaged in the same nonsense but with little to no concern about their health, work, money, family, friends, the police, the dope dealer, their home (many of us were homeless), or their main squeeze. Most of us couldn't care less about the community, or the neighborhood we lived in.

When we think it through for real and truly get "honest," for some of us it was a shock to our "thinking process" to experience even fleeting moments of clarity. This is the Madness of Addiction, in desperate need of Cognitive Restructuring.

~ x ~

Part One: Pockets of My History:
"Memories Can Be Out-Cold Sometimes"

Charles Fowlkes

Chapter 1: About the Author: "Them Older Cats"

I was born in Dyersburg Tenn., July 17,1954, in a little house on Fair Street, but I was raised in the city of Detroit in a place called the Jefferies Projects, better known as the "Yard" (a penitentiary euphemism).

At the tender age of 12 or 13, I was asked by my big brother, Martin, along with a few other older cats, if I knew why the place, we called home was labeled a "project." My response was, "Tell me what's happening."

Martin explained to me that, if you looked down on the Projects from up above, it resembled a maze that rats run through, developed by the "powers that be."

I didn't understand none of that, all I knew was that the Projects was my home, and where I acquired an understanding of the bittersweet struggle of responsibility; the pain, fear, and secrecy of childhood trauma; religion; the excitement and cool of the impressionable age; the "madness of addiction"; multiple deaths in the family; and the differing views, opinions, and conjectures about growing into manhood.

What I'm about to lay on you was a bit much for my brain at the tender age mentioned above, but I'm gonna do my best to give it to you like they gave it to me.

I knew about the violence; I'd heard about the American Dream—but the *totality* of what they laid on me was most disturbing, not to mention the fact that growing up in the '60s, in the Projects, was pretty damn interesting, let me tell you! Them older cats had me spinning. Check out what they dropped on me next.

"Don't forget about kick the can, hide and seek (which later turned into hide and go get it), tag, root the peg, all the "balls" (base-, foot-, and basket), manhunt, four corners—and don't act like you never played hopscotch and jacks with the girls; never forget about your childhood, no matter what. You dig?"

I nodded my head to indicate "yes," but I didn't expect them to say that to me; I was still thinking about the "powers that be" and wanted them to tell me about that, but my brother told me, "Hold on; we gonna kick it about that in a minute."

It got heavy. I was lost for real. Check out what they told me.

They spoke about this other side of "Dark Truth"—that the Projects were set up as an "unpredictable homicide move" that we perpetrated on each other. A stress-filled chaotic maze, or "experiment," contrived by the "powers that be" to observe people in congested environments.

Can you imagine the expression that came across my face? Without words, it was "Huh?"

My understanding was zero, but that brother of mine came to my rescue. He told me not to get all bent up out of shape, because a lot of folks formed true friendships for real; he spoke about my friends, and how there was a lot of love flowing from a whole bunch of families in the Projects. He told me to hold on to that truth.

The other cats didn't let up on me, though. They told me to pay attention to the violent crimes—the anger and despair around me—like murder, sticking folks up, drinking like crazy that often led to violent encounters, slanging drugs, abusing drugs, and how some folks committed suicide to escape their present reality. They spoke about this massive waste of life, not only in the Projects but around the world—that it was necessary to prevent overpopulation, that war was necessary, that there would always be the haves and the have nots, and the American Dream was one of the greatest lies ever told.

Like I said, I was lost for real—all that talk about overpopulation, war being necessary, the "powers that be"—I was clueless!

I was okay with American Dream because I'd heard about that in school, and from some other folks in the Projects who had told me that we *all* could get a piece of the "Dream"!

The older cats cut off my train of thought, and asked me about the American Dream: did I think or believe that it applied to "all" black folks. Were they reading my mind or something?

I told them that I thought it did, but this was from listening to folks talking about the big pretty house, the white picket fence, a car or two in the driveway, and a whole lot of money in the bank.

They just laughed. I didn't see "anything" funny about what I said, but they weren't laughing at me, though. Check out what they told me.

They told me that the "powers that be" will make sure that a host of black folks and other people of color strike it rich as athletes, entertainers, lawyers, doctors, judges, etc.—just to make it look good and create the *illusion* that anybody could attain riches. As for what them other folks had told me about the "Dream" applying to everybody—they told me, "It didn't."

The older cats told me about some kind of "class set-up" and folks being placed into "categories." This, they said, came from the mind of "super-rich white folks," the "powers that be."

I said it real loud (I think I scared myself a little bit): "White people, white folks doing this?"]

Yes, they told me, and with their immense wealth they put in place sociologists, psychotherapists, behavioral therapists, psychometrics, scientists from all fields of knowledge, as well as the leading architects to design and create a maze-like home setting for people of color, with just a slight difference in structural concept for those who would forever remain "middle class." A setting where wine, beer, liquor stores were strategically placed for continuous consumption, and drugs were available from dope houses up the street, around the corner and down the block.

On a much grander scale, the older cats told me about the intellectual prowess of certain men/women, employed by the powers that be, to devise the wickedness of feeding "specific groups of people" hate propaganda, war and race domination, all while a whole bunch of folks were going after and trying to hold on to as much peace, love, and happiness as they could—peace, love, and happiness that the American Dream claimed was ours to pursue.

This was like the "Genesis of My World View," but was it a lie, or was truth being told, because the older cats who laid all of this powerful information on me were dope fiends, straight up!

It was through memory and research when I got much older that I can even spell, let alone know, the meaning of the words they used in their spiel about white folks. During my teenage years, my brother tried to help me understand most of what was said, but I still didn't get it all the way.

Now I understand why, when I was between the ages of 14 and 16, he had me *try* to read books by Eric Fromm, Carl Jung, B.F. Skinner, Nathaniel Branden, Thomas Szasz. Let me break it down all the way for you. I went from *Fun with Dick and Jane* ("See Spot Run") to *Grimm's Fairy Tales*, Mark Twain's *Adventures of Huckleberry Finn, Great Expectation*" by Charles Dickens, *Pimp: The Story of My Life* and *The Naked Soul of Iceberg Slim*, both by Robert Beck, and the authors mentioned above. I was straight-up tripping when he had me listening to an album about "Sidney Poitier Meets Plato," for real!

He laid a lot of heavy stuff on me, like when he told me about that "hate whitey" nonsense—that hate was a waste of mental energy, and there's no intellectual benefit involved. Nonetheless, it was the beginning of a particular mind-set about white folks and a rebellious attitude.

Pockets of my history.

Chapter 2: "The "Root Causes"

- The Genesis of My World View (Chapter One)
- Childhood Trauma
- The Excitement and Cool of the Impressionable Age
- Multiple Deaths in the Family. (This was the continuing saga in my extended tour in the "madness of addiction.")

Childhood Trauma

Picture me at 10 or 11 years old. This part of my life has been suppressed for so long that, when I try to bring this nonsense that my brother-ln-law did to me back into some kind of clear focus, all I get is "Snapshots"; there are no connecting events that I can recall in the order of occurrence.

First Snapshot: he was a tall man, black as midnight and scary as hell when he was drunk; he was married to my sister.

2nd Snapshot, he made me play and fondle with his genitals, snatched my pants, my underwear down around my ankles and fondled me as well. These memories are cloudy concerning location, I vaguely remember some bushes, a small room—I really don't remember. What I do know is that it happened more than once, I can hear his words in my mind and the deafening sound of a slap upside my head. "If you tell anybody, boy, I swear I'm gonna hurt you real bad; you understand me?"

The Excitement and Cool of the Impressionable Age:

I Remember

I remember watching them older cats in their stingy brims, silk mohair suits, parkers, hi-lows, alligator shoes, them Stetsons—and one cat with a black cape on and turban to match, with what looked like a diamond sitting right in the front of his turban.

I remember sitting on the basement steps in the Projects when I was 11 or 12, watching a small group of men/women getting high in their silk underwear, listening to jazz—and the ladies were damn near butt naked; I couldn't wait to get some silk drawers, stick a joint in my mouth and talk smack for real!

I remember standing in front of the mirror in my room, going through the motions, mimicking the behavior of the older cats. I was picturing in my mind how to conduct myself, what I would say when I stepped out on the stage of the street to get my imaginary hustle on; thoroughly engaged and ready for my curtain call with the alibis, the fake tears, and rehearsed magical lies. I know there's somebody reading this who can truly identify!

Multiple Deaths in the Family:

My Mama.

In the year 2000, I, along with a few other family members, found mama dead on her kitchen floor from a heart attack, with hole in her head from hitting the bottom of her old-style kitchen table. She lived in the tall Projects when you cross the bridge on the 13th floor.

When I think back on that horrific day, I can still hear the sound of breaking skin, bone crushing against metal, just as I did when sat on the floor next to her.

Now check out my sick thinking on the floor with my mama. I was devastated by her death, but what went through my head was how now she wouldn't be able to give me the 20-25 dollars I was gonna ask her for. Don't get it twisted, I love my mama, but, at the age of 44-45, which is how old I was when we found mama dead, I was a crack-head, a drunk, a criminal, a terrible father; I was all out of pocket for real!

Enough of that, we gonna shift gears for a minute and kick it about "life." Stay with me.

Watch this here: my mama was a short, cute brown-skinned woman, and she would say all the time, "I'm small, but I'm well put together!" She was a little jazzy for real.

I remember when I was just a little fella; I would walk mama to the bus stop early in the morning; she worked at Sinai hospital. Looking up at my mama while we were waiting on the bus, I saw a smile on her face that put a smile on my face, and I know now that she was proud of herself for making her own money and not having to depend on my distant invisible father. I learned from Cognitive Restructuring that I don't have to stay in the "bad place"; I can move on, changing my thinking and behavior. I love my mama; I miss her so much.

Nita

In the year 2001, my wife Nita had a stroke in front of me, but it didn't register right-away because I was so high and out of my mind. Two weeks later, she had a heart attack and died. This was overwhelmingly disturbing; I was still tripping about my mama.

Let me kick it about Nita like this here. There was a whole lot of love and many years with this pretty Indian black woman, and back in the day we had it going on in the Projects, let me tell you!

She laid some wisdom down on the brother; let me drop a sample. She was all the way "live" in the weed game, and we made a few dollars, (a lot of dollars); we were "Ghetto-Hood Rich" for real!

I remember when she told me about the "appropriate interaction" with your woman when she's feeling a certain type of way (I'm not talking about her "monthlies") and she has to throw hints or play a role because you don't pick up on it. Learning how to read your woman for real! I learned so much from this girl, and, to tell you the truth, I never thought she would be interested in a guy like me because, when we originally met, I was out of mind!

You couldn't tell me that my communication skills weren't a hit with the ladies; I thought I was a player for real with my herculean chest, that pretty singing voice that God blessed me with, and my jerry-curl hairstyle; I thought I was that guy!

She obviously saw something in the brother because we connected for real. Hold on—Nita, too, was blessed with a powerful singing voice (and no doubt this was one of the many reasons for the attraction); she had this range that was phenomenal, and it was a joy to see the children looking at their mama while she was singing, with that big old smile on their faces. She was a hell of a woman for sho'!

Billie (My Middle Brother)

He was my storyteller, my Santa Claus, and he called himself "Creamy Big Daddy"! He took a turn for the worse, though, dealing with a severe mental disorder. He balled up in a fetal position and passed on from renal failure, complicated by his Acute Paranoid Schizophrenia. I love this man with all my heart!

Katherine, My Oldest Sister

I didn't get a chance to kick it with her like I wanted to. Only specific events stick out in my mind (like they do about Billie), but I'm not going there; that's straight up personal!

I'll share this with you: they both suffered from the same mental disorder. Memories of them both provided a blueprint for me because, when I moved to Madison, Wisconsin, that was the field of work that I engaged in—substance abuse and mental health. I love my big sister without a doubt!

Martin, My Oldest Brother

Don't get it twisted about that dope-fiend comment a few minutes ago. My brother was highly intelligent; he was streetwise savvy, and he laid down a "subtle command performance" in the Projects, which elevated that last name "Fowlkes" to an extreme level of importance. For confirmation ask my Young Lion Chucky!

It's sad that he was caught up in the madness of addiction in an ugly sort of way; he passed in September of 2011, while I was living in Madison. I went back to Detroit; I had to perform the eulogy, I got through it, but it was troubling for the brother on so many levels. I love this cat for real!

My Brother-in-Law, C. J.

Two words from this man prepared me for "continued survival": "No Fear!" It took a long time for me to understand all of what was involved in embracing "no fear," but it finally happened for me with true-life experiences in the Projects and beyond. Genuine hustler C. J. was "Taurus the Bull" for real but laid down a demonstration of love for his family that in my humble opinion surprised a lot of folks. My love for C. J. is Constant and Sure.

My Niece, the Lovely Michelle

Hell of a woman, hell of mama, with that "Glistening Smile" that made everybody around her happy—do you feel what I'm saying? I love my niece; I miss my niece for real!

My Mother-in-Law, Sarah

She was my heart and kept it real with the brother at all times, especially when I was caught up in the madness; she laid the law down on the brother for real! I will always love my "Sarah Smile," believe that!

My Father, Martin

His going-home celebration occurred long before the other members in the family, but I really didn't know him. I guess I'm supposed to feel some kind of way about him because he's my father, but I gotta keep it real with you. I wish we had more "father/son time" together, but that's as far as I can go with it. The love for him is based on his participation in bringing about the baby named Charles.

My Sister Vern

Unexpected for real! I call her "Pops" because of her big pretty eyes! My sister would want it to be "known" that she embraced the "Gospel of the Grace of God"! The Gospel revealed to Paul from the "Heavenly Yeshua"! I Love My Pops! Woo-Wee!

The pain I just shared is throughout the "recovering community" and a whole bunch of folks on the planet. But a lot of us put our big-boy drawers on—big girl panties on— doing what we "need to do," and sometimes what we "want to do," because keeping it real is not a struggle no mo'!

We got something to talk about, and we know beyond a shadow of doubt that we're a "Work in Progress," because there's a lot of "learning and unlearning" to do—do you feel what I'm saying? I got one more "Pocket" to lay on you to bring around this full circle. I had to embrace the "Reality of a Made-up Mind, and a Commitment to Excellence"!

Chapter 3: "To the Professionals"

This "Vision" of "True Connections," Responsible Adults for Tomorrow, was birthed from personal experience, I don't have a Bachelor's, Master's or Ph. D. I did however acquire a SAC-IT, (Substance Abuse Counselor in Training), and I'm truly grateful to the Minority Counselor Training Institute and Hope Haven's treatment facility, for the knowledge I received was most valuable indeed.

It would be remiss of me not to speak about the professionals who labored tirelessly to acquire the prestigious degrees mentioned above, and Mr. Robert Beck can stand amongst these professionals with a Ph. D in "Street-ology" for real!

Trust me, I haven't taken leave of my senses, I have the utmost respect for these accomplished authors, the "Giants" in the field of "addiction and behavioral issues": Stanton Peele, Archie Brodsky, Mary Arnold, David J. Powell, William L. White, Vince Fox, Herbert Fingarette, Pat Denning, Jeannie Little, Tina B. Tessina, Charlotte Davis Kasl, Bruce Alexander Albert Ellis, Nathaniel Branden, Thomas Szasz, and many more. It's time for the recovering community to feast on this vast treasure chest of wisdom and penetrating insight into addiction and how to overcome destructive thinking and behavior. To the professionals, I humbly acknowledge their enormous achievements, and my respect is real.

Therapist/Counselor and Client Achieved a "True Connection"

"True Connections" get down like this here. We believe and stand on the fact that it's an individual choice to embrace whatever you "feel" and have "thought through" that works for you. AA, NA, Smart Recovery, the Church, or how "True

Connections" operate, with a "Powerful Personal Decision" to end the madness in your life—whatever works for you

"Work It"! There are many more support groups/agencies/avenues to pursue throughout the community and beyond. Personally, I no longer embrace the disease concept of addiction and the ever-so-popular 12 Step Program, and my reasons for this disconnect will be expressed in the "10 Connections."

This "True Connections" alternative, this "Men and Women Empowerment Group" is presented with that butt-naked, in-the-raw, true-to-life approach from the "madness of addiction," interwoven with Cognitive Restructuring. A psychotherapeutic process of learning how to identify and dispute maladaptive thoughts, such as all-or-nothing thinking, filtering, over-generalizations, magical thinking, magnification, and emotional reasoning.

All that definition for me was broken down like this here. It took me a while to understand the wisdom of talking with "somebody" about all that death in the family, and my brother-in-law's nonsense. To this day I still be tripping about not telling my brothers what he did to me; boy, that fear can paralyze you and prevent you from doing the right thing for the right reason, let me tell you!

It finally happened for me, I started "Listening for Real" to specific therapist counselors who took a stand with Cognitive Behavioral Therapy. This "listening experience" occurred when I moved to Madison, Wisconsin, in 2006, but I first heard about this process in 2003 or 2004 in a facility called "Elmhurst Home," located on two of the many dangerous streets on the West Side of Detroit, Linwood and Elmhurst. I will speak more about this experience under the heading "On a Personal Note."

Along with "listening" was the reading and study of more than a few books and journals written by the "Giants" mentioned above, and I embarked on a thought-provoking journey of trying to bring my "past" back into as much of a clear focus as I could—from events and situations (not all bad; I had a slew of good times, for real!) to my crazy thoughts about religion and relationships (family and community); the confusion of belief in God, the Devil, and that Bible; alcohol and other drugs; and particular individuals who caused pain and/or discomfort in my life.

Discovery was eye opening. Like so many others I had formed a "belief system" based on "other folks' teachings"—what they felt and thought to be "the truth" (family and community)—check it out. I was still holding on to the belief that I suffered from the disease of addiction. I was praying to God for deliverance without an understanding that I had to work in harmony with the prayer. There was no "human responsibility"; I was expecting God to do everything for me. I was not aware that I was engaging in what I later learned to be "destructive coping skills." I had no knowledge of the grieving process, Post Traumatic Stress Disorder—none of that! I got high and tried to stay high on a daily basis.

Thinking back on it now, I sincerely believe that I was emulating the behavior of the older cats in the Projects because I wanted to be just like my brother Martin for real! "The Excitement and Cool of the Impressionable Age."

Chapter 4: "Brand New Day for the Brother Now"

Brand new day for the brother now, and I understand the "restructuring process," I can "sift through, identify, and remove all that Negative Scary Stuff" from my belief system. I can truly appreciate my brother Martin for his insistence on having me read on a daily basis, even what he had me "trying" to read.

Reflections on the counseling staff at Elmhurst Home's treatment setting in Detroit, even though it was a short stay for the brother: one of the counselors put it on the floor for real; check him out. "You're a soldier under construction, not "destruction; you got it twisted! I see you got some entertainer in you. Just so you know, it's all right to shine, as long as you shine appropriately." Do you feel what he said to me?

The move from Detroit to Madison was just what the doctor ordered. At Hope Haven's treatment facility, Journey Mental Health "Men's Trauma Group"—from all that "listening and deep-down honest reflection" that I spoke about in "Word to the Reader"—the appropriate application was thoroughly discussed.

- A "practice" of grounding skills, relaxation skills, establishing appropriate boundaries, paying attention to my body signals whenever I sense the anger or the sadness swelling up inside and know that this can lead to violent behavior brought on by the anger or overwhelming depression brought on by the sadness; an awareness of "emotional responses to memories."
- Understanding that trauma and substance-abuse interaction was crucial, because all of them major scary-ass flashbacks were driving the brother stone crazy for real!

- The profound understanding that I am no longer entangled, no longer in bed with the insanity of how I conducted myself in my "yesterday."

Therapist counselor and client achieved a "True Connection," I was "visible"; there was demonstration of genuine concern.

Now, watch this here: if you feel like you have to, want to, or are prompted by family/friends to see a professional, make sure that he or she will "talk with you," and "not talk at you"—do you feel what I'm saying?

Chapter 5: "It's Time to Shake Things Up for Real!" Can We Continue?

This manuscript is designed to assist those just starting out in their recovery process, as well as to advise the "so many" still caught up in the madness that it's time to stop being lazy when it comes to "thinking."

It's time to develop a plan of action—a strategy, if you will—that involves the "awakening of the productive individual" inside the crack-head, the drunk, the criminal, the whore, certain trauma folks, intravenous drug users, and those who nurse their "twins," excessively snorting cocaine, heroin, hydrocodone, meth, Tylenol—and some folks who might have tried snorting Bayer Aspirin and Ibuprofen too, Stop It!

Everybody on the planet knows that these individuals are not restricted to the "hood"; this applies to the judges secretly drinking in their chambers as frequently as they can; the lawyer who thinks no one knows about his cocaine expenses and his obsession with ladies of the night; the doctor caught up in lie after lie to her husband and children about her gambling debt. I can go on and on, but, in harmony with the "doc" point, seen money won!

Every now and then it surfaces on TV about an entertainer or some other professional caught up in the madness, and their behavior is always associated with the disease concept of addiction.

Let me drop it like this here for "everybody still caught up in it." *You* are responsible for any present or future acts of crime and just straight-up stupidity that you commit, but you wanna cast it off and speak to that lie, "I have a disease, I can't help it"!

Can we continue embracing this nonsense? Can we continue with the absurdity of in-and-out-of-jail, in-and-out-of-programs, with frequent trips to the penitentiary? Can we continue subjecting ourselves to a "series of treatment visits" over and over again? Can we continue in unhealthy abusive relationships out of fear? Writing goodbye letters to our addictions, and sitting around support groups that kick it about the disease of addiction like it's a fact; and telling folks that they will be in recovery forever?

The present dinosaur existence of diseased-based treatment programs will always have a place in the recovering community. I'm writing this to serve notice that "True Connections" will arise and breathe new life into the community, that plan of action, that strategy is Cognitive Restructuring, presented with that butt-naked, in-the-raw, true-to-life approach from the madness of addiction; it's time to "Shake Things Up for Real"!

I get it. I understand the wisdom associated with the soothing professional discourse in trauma groups and various recovery settings, because of the possible danger of triggering someone's traumatic experience. This "True Connections" but naked in-the-raw approach might be a bit much for some folks, and that's okay. Stick to what you know. Just know that "True Connections" is here for you when you need a dose of inspiration and motivation.

Now let me touch on Cognitive Restructuring a little bit mo' for you. It will challenge and open up recovering minds to the wisdom/the reality of psychological freedom, no longer enmeshed in doctrines that suffocate the life out of you! A true embrace with self-responsibility, the "joy of thinking," learning how to think things through, and so much more. Now watch this here; I know some of you know about that "Shake-Things-Up approach" because you know that "Soft-Ass approach" hasn't been working out for you. Keep it 100 with yourself first!

Chapter 6: Before I Proceed... "Let's Kick It about Addiction and the Madness of Addiction"

Addiction. Using their expertise, substance-abuse counselors, physiologist, neuroscientists, and a host of professionals have expounded upon the meaning of this word. I sincerely believe that "some folks" in the recovering community, as well as other folks on the planet, deal with "acceptance fatigue" when it comes to what they believe to be true or not.

Like I said before, we all have "addictions." I'm talking about the excessive, destructive indulgence with a substance, activity, or whatever! Check it out: gardening, jogging, listening to music, using that phone, reading those books, letting your obsession with that man/that woman keep you up all night, or claiming that it tastes so good, it feels so good, that it's hard for me to stop (which applies to sex, food drugs, and what I started out with—personally, I'm addicted to books, but I don't suffer from the disease of "book-ism"; my behavior is not out of control). It's extremely sad that this word, addiction, is always associated with something "bad and ugly" because that's simply not true.

Watch this here—you're on the phone in your room with little to no interaction with family or playing a video game for hours and hours on a daily basis so that sometimes you're late for work, not washing your ass, not eating right. *That's* the "Madness of Addiction"; that's not a "disease." Stop It! Such thinking means you're in desperate need of Cognitive Restructuring.

My take on it is like this here: Addiction is thinking and behavior about *something* that you like to do a lot of for real, *consistently.* My/your "past reality, "present reality" provides a wealth of information about our habits, because there is much to learn from the positive and or negative impact of environment, family, and community during what many professionals call the "formative years." Check it out. Trauma from child molestation (past reality) or the death of a family member or friend (present reality or combination of past and present) often culminates in extreme substance abuse for a whole lot of folks. There's that "something," (cocaine, heroin, drunkenness, etc.)

The acquisition of large sums of money from hustling in the streets is an exhilarating experience that floods both mind and body. When that "something" that you keep on doing becomes excessive and destructive, it's time to change your thinking and behavior for real! I'm not about to throw a monkey wrench in it with talk about having a "disease." Stop It!

It's time for a Powerful Personal Decision to end the madness in your life; you got to know that you can join in with the massive flow of folks who have stopped smoking crack, snorting cocaine, shooting heroin, committing criminal nonsense—who are no longer drinking excessively or gambling excessively (who've maybe just stopped altogether)—those certain trauma folks who demonstrate the *intellectual awareness*, the *readiness*, to acquire the necessary positive life skills/coping skills. And hats off to those individuals who are no longer sitting around zombie-like from smoking that weed. This is not rocket science; any substance/activity taken to a level of excessive, destructive indulgence is just straight-up insane—believe that!

I don't have it twisted, I know we all got a say-so in how we process our view(s) on addiction and recovery; let me bring mine home for you. We all engaged in a "restructuring process." It's talked about at the meetings that a lot of folks attend. It's probably not expressed that way (as a "restructuring process"), but that's what it is when we think about "People, Places, and Things"; we have to *restructure our thinking.*

For some folks restructuring their thinking was a hard row to hoe. They found themselves going back to the drawing board, so to speak, holding on to what had been "familiar" for so long. And some folks couldn't "shake the place" where the "pain took place," nor the individual(s) who inflicted it.

A lot of us mixed it up—AA, NA, and the Church; Individual Therapy, Trauma Groups, AA, and the Church; Meditation Groups/Mindfulness Groups, Expensive Get-Aways, etc. We were thoroughly committed to finding some kind of "healthy balance," and it was not only time consuming, but, for a lot of folks, it was elusive as hell! Do you feel what I'm saying? Now I want you to check out the list that will be discussed in the following chapters.

Part Two: "The TEN Connections"

A Serious and Closer Look: Connections 1 & 2 (Chapter 7)

The List:

- Listening For Real
- Understand the Root Causes
- Listen and Participate in Some Deep-Down Honest Reflection
- A Continuum of Ins and Outs
- Powerful Personal Decision
- Willing to Put the Work In!
- Butt-Naked Honesty
- Self-Talk Adventures
- Straight-up Love for You

Discovering the Truth about Ourselves/Internal Inspection: Connection 3 (Chapter 8)

"At Some Point"! Connections 4 through 9 (Chapter 9)

- Learning How to Think Things Through
- Sift Through, Identify, and Remove That Negative Scary Stuff
- From an Overload of Negative Reactions to Developing a Proactive Mind-Set
- Standing on My Own Two Feet for Real!
- Challenge from Within
- Bondage
- Self-Defeat
- Make It Make Sense, and, If You Can't, Stop It!
- A Soldier under Construction, not Destruction, I had It Twisted, but "Not No Mo"!
- Bullet Proof Thinking
- We are Winners!

"No Longer Trapped in "Still", the 10th Connection Embrace the Reality of a Made-up Mind and a Commitment to Excellence! (Chapter 10)

Charles Fowlkes

Chapter 7: The FIRST & SECOND Connection: A Serious and Closer Look

The FIRST Connection

Some of us in the recovering community started "Listening for Real" to specific therapists, counselors or particular family members/particular friends who loved us and wanted us to be successful in whatever we wanted to achieve and who would call us out on BS every time!

Many of us wanted first of all to truly "Understand the Root Causes"—you know, the "why of it all"—and we eventually made a decision to "Listen and Participate in some Deep-Down Honest Reflection." We took a serious and closer look at our belief system, our addiction(s), our world view, and the role that drinking, drugging, slanging, etc., played in our lives—and considered what impact (positive or negative) our internal and external environment and our upbringing had on our lives.

We discovered that, for many of us, growing up was heart wrenching (incest, drunkenness, and violence in the home; physical, mental, emotional abuse)—just straight-up chaotic! Many of us embraced a "Continuum of Ins and Outs," in and out of jail, in and out of programs, in and out of abusive relationships—it went on and on.

Some of us though, made a Powerful Personal Decision to end the madness in our lives and came face to face with a profound truth. In harmony with this decision, we recognized that we "needed help"—and the strength, courage, understanding, and inner fortitude, came from many sources depending on the individual. For some of us it was the God of Scripture, for others it was "Female Entities" or going to meetings—or a pastor, sponsor, mentor, PO, drug counselor, therapist, wife, husband, main squeeze, or children (those "specific individuals" I spoke about above).

The "restructuring process" was not an easy task, but we were committed to changing our destructive thinking and behavior—we *had to*! Now, watch this here: alcoholics, crack heads, intravenous drug users, certain trauma folks, criminals and whores, are some of the greatest thinkers, for real! That's why, when they were no longer caught up in the "madness of addiction," they laid down a solid strong foundation because they were "Willing to Put the Work In"!

The SECOND Connection

This Connection is contingent on "individual thought process," because a lot of folks couldn't handle that "Butt-Naked Honesty" right away or being called out on their BS; check it out.

We did our "Listening for Real" (professionals call this "Active Listening") while others were in consultation with their "entity of choice." Eventually they called us out for all of our insane thinking and behavior; they called us out for real!

Some of us, though, had a different take on it, and a few of them expressed ideas that were just straight-up insane; check it out: "We can't afford to just quickly accept someone else's truth for our direction without evaluating the practical application to our situation." What the hell is that? Does it sound intelligent and wise to you? That's straight-up nonsense! Here we are, "stuck on stupid"—some of us for a decade or mo'—and we get called out on our BS and wanna act like we're "Brand New"? Stop It!

It's not a mystery that a lot of us disconnected from the truth in a mighty way and told so many lies it's a wonder we didn't self-implode! This truth is mind boggling, and it really hurt deep down inside to know how much pain and worry we laid on our families. Many of us asked ourselves on so many "Self-Talk Adventures," "Can we continue in this miserable existence? In and out of jail, in and out of programs, accepting black eyes and swollen lips, hitting licks and turning tricks?"

Listen up, baby boy, baby girl, you don't have to lick nothing, suck nothing—stop all that flat-backing, and get up off your knees doggie styling for a few rocks of crack cocaine, money, or some blow; truly, my brother, my sister, you don't have to be a whore no mo', unless you're just cut like that.

To my brothers, my sisters—stop allowing your mind to kick it persuasively with your "monkey," your "mouth," your "ass," to keep on putting your life at risk. I hope none of you are turning dates at the crib around your children, because you know that's nasty as hell and so disrespectful Stop It! Everything I'm saying is just "Straight-up Love for You," believe that!

Chapter 8: The THIRD Connection: "Discovering the Truth about Ourselves/Internal Inspection"

Discovering the truth about ourselves was pretty damn interesting and a little scary (a lot of scary for some of us). Childhood trauma, neglect, single-parent homes—though I'm pretty sure that a whole lot of folks were raised with the appropriate discipline and structure, and with much love, but some of those young adults still got caught up in the madness; what was missing? Nothing!

It's like the lyrical genius of Sly and the Family Stone, with their masterpiece "It's a Family Affair." Check out this snippet of profound truth: "One child grows up to be / somebody that just loves to learn. / Another child grows up to be / somebody that you'd just love to burn!"

Do you feel what Sly and the Family Stone are saying? It is what it is! Some of us were exposed to the streets at an early age—perhaps growing up in a dope house, or perhaps our parents/guardians were dope fiends and drunks—and we saw a lot of ugly going down. Learning how to think it through was a daunting task, painful sometimes, but eventually we "internalized the truth."

Discovering this truth was an eye-opening experience; we came to understand that "any discovery of truth" about ourselves is subject to change as we "grow or don't grow in wisdom and discernment." The truth was/is mind blowing for a lot of us; we were scared as hell, and we had to tell all of that "fear inside" to kiss our ass for real!

We were not the perpetrators here, we did not "initiate the pain," and wearing that "victim-stance outfit" for all those years drove a lot of us into trauma groups, individual therapy, extreme substance abuse, etc. We finally achieved a level of confidence in our thinking, recognizing that "troublesome thoughts and scary feelings" will arise during this "Internal Inspection," but we can't allow the wreckage, the pain of our past to continue bleeding into our present and contaminating our future—do you feel what I'm saying?

What I went through is an experience shared throughout the recovering community. I didn't corner the market on pain, and I don't have it twisted! I know that we're not on top of our game 24/7, but we damn sho' can be "consistently positive" as best we can; this is the order for every day!

Chapter 9: At Some Point!
Connections FOUR thru NINE

The FOURTH Connection

Learning how to Think Things Through became the norm in our mental process, but by no means did we always negotiate it successfully! The "restructuring process" of learning how to "sift through, identify, and remove all of that Negative Scary Stuff from our belief system" was a monumental task, but, at some point, we had to meet the challenge head on! From an "Overload of Negative Reactions" to the joys and challenges of life, we began to truly understand the need for a "Proactive Mind-Set" in every area of our life. We began the process of "thought selection," concerning ourselves with the thinking and behavior that relates to the following:

- Drugs, (slanging, abusing, street, and prescription
- The Pain, Fear and Secrecy of Childhood Trauma
- Pursuing Sexual Encounters one after another—Stop It!
- Gambling, Shopping, that Phone, etc.
- Jealousy
- Relationships
- Mama and Daddy
- Children
- Your Main Squeeze
- Community

We were ready to embrace the process of Cognitive Restructuring, the invaluable assistance in overcoming destructive thinking and behavior; with a true understanding of "individual circumstance." Therapy and trauma groups just may be the launching pad for take-off with the embrace of Cognitive Restructuring.

The "Restructuring Process—Think and Behave":

- Think and Behave about Yourself: Personal hygiene and spiritual, intellectual, emotional, financial growth is that your plan of action? Do you really care about how you smell? How you look? The "Presentation of Self?"

- Think and Behave about Your Home/Apt: How are you living? If there is a problem with personal upkeep in the place where you dream, fart with abandonment, make plans with family and friends, scratch yourself like you really want to, etc.—if there is a problem, you need to address that situation with a strong sense of urgency! Is your home *still* set up for those caught up in the madness—even though you're sharing at the meeting that it's dangerous for you to congregate with those folks? You can't keep it 100% with yourself? Recovering Community, *Pay Attention!*

- Think and Behave—about Money: Isn't this a "No Brainer?"

- Think and Behave—about Alcohol and other Drugs.

- Think and Behave—about Your Wife, Husband, Your Main Squeeze, Your Children.

- Think and Behave—about Interactions with Family and folks in the Community: This is of paramount importance because the Appropriate Discipline, Constructive Role Models, and Family Discussions in the Home, are the result of "Effective

Communication Skills." There are no guarantees; we just put events in motion!

- Think and Behave—about "total abstinence as a choice," not the "struggle of a lifetime," Stop It and Knock It Off!

- The Awakening of the Productive Individual

The FIFTH Connection

At some point, I had to come to a profound understanding that, throughout my journey as a responsible adult, I can't have my therapist, sponsor, mentor, my mellow, my parents, or whoever "still holding my hand"! I had to realize and seriously embrace the "true connection" of the wisdom and strength of character that flows from "Standing on My Own Two Feet for Real"!

The SIXTH Connection

For some of us in the recovering community, it was becoming a "Challenge from Within," and we could no longer be joined at the hip with the belief that, "once you're an alcoholic you're always an alcoholic, and, once you're an addict, you're always an addict."

This negative label is akin to "Bondage," and, when we kicked it with other folks in the recovering community, the label didn't last long because they were convinced that we were in serious trouble if we didn't rethink our position.

Let me drop it like this here on you. Our stand is drenched in courage, in psychological freedom, and we will no longer tolerate nor consume "doctrines of fatalism," which are a continuous embrace of "Self-Defeat." We will no longer engage in that excessive, destructive indulgence with mood-changing-mind altering-chemicals or activities; we will not put the folks that we truly love through that nonsense "no mo"! Do you feel what I'm saying?

Now check this out. You went through a five-year bit, but now you're 12 years jail free. Your history may reveal some criminal behavior, or maybe you were falsely accused and had to do the time anyway; it happens sometimes. For other folks, their history is true to form concerning their criminal/incarceration behavior.

The point is this here. Now that you're 12 years jail free, penitentiary free, are you still a criminal? Will you call yourself out like that at a meeting, the way other folks call themselves "addicts and alcoholics"? What's the point? I don't see the wisdom in it because it's counter-productive; the purpose is zero in substance!

We're a "Work in Progress," without a doubt, but the progress is moving forward, constructive—challenging to be sure, but we stand with confidence that we can and will pull it off! Not like "other folks" with this "robust affirmation" about a substance/activity that you haven't engaged in for 12 years but your "disease is still progressing"? "Make it Make Sense, and, if you can't, Stop It!"

The SEVENTH Connection

The thinking about a support group is that we have to research its foundation and examine its purpose; we can no longer be of the mind-set that would have us "settle"; it's time to stop being lazy when it comes to "thinking."

Don't get this twisted—this is not an "over examination of ourselves"; you pick your own time frame, day/days, and frequency as to how you handle yours. We have to stay connected to our truth to hold ourselves accountable for what we say and do. That's not easy for a lot of folks because it's not a mystery that a whole bunch of folks suffer from PTSD, which varies in diagnosis.

Different levels of mental retardation—mild, moderate, severe—as well as serious painful physical conditions oftentimes cripple our ability to be true to ourselves and others. My take on it is like this here: I'm a Soldier under Construction, not "destruction," for the rest of my life. I had it twisted but not "no mo"!

Watch this here: this life-changing experience is not for cowards or spineless individuals, nor for those who think it's a badge of honor to be locked down in the penitentiary. I shot a move from Detroit to Madison because I had to put an end to all that unnecessary whining, feeling sorry for myself, and that sorry ass thinking that I'm a lost cause in order to "Step Into My New Life For Real"! This is for those who know they can get their act together, and who *know* they can. Stop playing! Trust me, cowards don't engage in this; they're in a solid love affair with excuses.

The EIGHTH Connection

We raised the level of our self-esteem, with an intense awareness that we have to keep it real in our "personal assessment" of ourselves—especially when we know that we're laying it down real good.

Check it out. On time for work and not slacking when you get there, spending quality with family, creating and maintaining genuine friendships, keeping the home fire burning, and taking out some "me time" for yourself.

The flipside comes into play, without a doubt, because we will experience those bad days, afternoons, early evenings, and midnight too! Most of us got a therapist, pastor, main squeeze, brother/sister from another mother, or a strong loving family member to help us through it. We can't afford to fake ourselves out by thinking that we're "Bullet Proof" just because we had a few good days, several months, or even a good year—but we can take "ownership" of the desired change we need or want in our lives, I'm just speaking truth to you.

The NINTH Connection

Now we can finally stand on the fact that we don't have to get wasted, trashed, or otherwise "negatively respond" in order to deal with troublesome thoughts and scary feelings "No mo!"

For many of us, the "visual" of ourselves when we were caught up in the madness is heart-breaking. Check it out. Some of us were as thin as a blade of grass, while others were just fat, sloppy, nasty—just trifling as hell! There were some who, from being out in the madness, had a "collection of war wounds" that they tried to hide from family and "certain friends."

I'm gonna keep it 100 with you, 'cause I stepped up in the dope house many times like I was okay, but my "internal pain" showed up on my face regardless of the fake smiles and pretense. I got high and kicked it with the other dope-fiends in the crib like they were my assigned therapist because the truth is that, for many of us, those folks getting high at the spot were the only people we *could* kick it with, depending on individual circumstance.

I'm just telling it like it was and still is for some folks. Like I said from jump, this is that butt-naked, in-the-raw, true-to-life approach to the madness of addiction.

Wait a minute—I feel a "reader." Look, this is not about shaming anybody; this is keeping it real with your "own personal experience." If it doesn't apply to you, applaud yourself, but know that a lot of ugly went down for a whole bunch of folks caught up in the madness of addiction. Now we understand the intensity of the work ahead, through trials and starting over again many times for some of us, but we kept on "putting the work in" because, upon "honest reflection," we know that we held on for so long to the "pain of our yesterday"! "We are Winners"—believe that!

Chapter 10: The TENTH Connection:
"No Longer Trapped in STILL!"

We are no longer trapped in "Still" for whatever reason.

- Still smoking crack to tweak out childhood trauma.
- Still getting drunk because you can't get over the death of your mama.
- Still shooting heroin regardless of the pain and worry you cause to family and friends, not to mention the reality of a lethal overdose.
- Still accepting black eyes and swollen lips, walking down the street hand in hand with your man, listening to him tell you for the 100th time. "Baby, you know I'm sorry; I'm trying to work on my anger issues, I promise never to hit you again; I promise this time for real!" You look up with one good eye; you wanna smile but your grill all busted up, and you believe that lie all over again.
- Still involved with criminal behavior (and I know at some point you had to think about getting a job, acquire a legitimate skill and stop all that criminal nonsense!).
- Still having sex with anybody and everybody while mama, auntie, grandma (or in some cases "whoever") agreed to watch or had custody of your children because you were caught up in the madness. And, after a night of sexual madness, consuming a bucket of sperm, turning tricks, you kicked it with the family members mentioned above about spending more time with the children, and they granted you the opportunity for a while, however briefly.

Now check your ass out. You didn't have the decency to brush your teeth or, if you had some dentures in your mouth, to take 'em out and gargle a little bit, or just put some sugar in your mouth before kissing your children—*damn!*

Don't get this twisted and think that I'm talking about "women only"; this applies to a whole bunch of men, but a lot of them won't own up to it. You better keep it real all the way, because we are "No Longer Trapped in "Still" for whatever reason—do you feel what the brother saying?

Part Three: Wrap this Around Your Thinking for a Minute: "Automatic Response"

Charles Fowlkes

Chapter 11: The "Aftermath"

From the jump, let me drop some truth on you. I'm "still" caught up in that "automatic response" to cigarettes. In the morning when my feet hit the floor, after a meal, or just hanging out waiting on the bus.

Now, watch this here: I have experienced an "internalization of truth," because I don't have to resort to destructive thinking and behavior to deal with "troublesome thoughts and scary feelings" no mo'! I don't have to get high when I get angry no mo', because of sadness no mo', and I don't have to "go get one" out of boredom no mo'. Boredom is a lack of creative thinking, by the way.

You see what I'm talking about when you believe that you suffer from a disease? Everything mentioned above is a set-up for "automatic response" again and again. Stop torturing yourself like that! I don't have to get high because it's a sunny day, a cloudy day, or my dog gave me his paw for the first time—*woo-wee!* I'm sharpening my necessary positive life skills/coping skills, with a profound understanding that I will always remain a "Work in Progress"! Learning how to think things through is part of the "new normal," with a crystal-clear awareness of what I said before, that we don't always negotiate this process successfully, and I don't have it twisted, because I don't always think it through when it comes to anger, sadness, and other emotions.

But watch this here: I got 15 years of "non-compliance to that emotional get-high nonsense"—do you feel what the brother is saying? I desperately need to squash them cigarettes, though; trust me, it's gonna happen. Find out for real what "You're Standing For," because that "false connection to belief systems and people too" is like you're standing in the presence of Truth, but then turn away to see what Lie is doing. This is Butt-Naked Honesty!

Unequivocally

I left Detroit in February of 2006 on a mission to get my life back. I touched down in Madison sometime in the afternoon the following day. I was scared, confused, and wanted a drink so bad that I could taste the Wild Irish Rose, Crown Royal, and Paul Masson swirling around in my mouth. I didn't drink, and I believe it was due to the consistent thought that soared through my mind: "Connection with God, connection with God." I could hear the voices of my sisters Janet and Vern, encouraging me to get my act together before I wound up dead some place.

Like I said, I was scared, but I found a homeless shelter in downtown Madison, and that's where I spent my first 30 days. It was during my stay there that I found out about a treatment facility located not far from the shelter called Hope Haven. I called on a regular basis, and on March 31st I was accepted into their program. I was beat down, half- crazy, and messed up from the floor up! I was shut down for real; I was "Closed for Repairs."

Now watch this here: I can stand with or without the recovering community and express unequivocally that I used to be a crack-head, but not no mo'. I used to be a drunk, but not no mo'. I used to be a criminal, but not no mo'. I used to gamble excessively, but not no mo'. I used to disrespect women, but not no mo'. I am no longer at war with myself, the struggle is over! I want you to feel what I'm saying down in the marrow of your bones, sinew and tissue, all up in your inner workings, so that you can truly understand the "Reality of a Made-up Mind and a Commitment to Excellence"!

I went from being a crack-head to the Resident Manager of Colvin Manor. I went from being a drunk to the Minority Counselor Training Institute. I went from being a criminal to a Substance Abuse Counselor in Training, at the same facility where I started out as a "client."

There is outright joy in knowing that the madness is over! You know what I get from some folks? That I'm boastful, over confident, just all caught up in myself. Watch this here—I'm not involved in that nonsense because my Father who art in heaven didn't arouse the thinking of a "wimp"! I understand the wisdom of "humble to remain teachable." I had to reintroduce myself to myself, from crack-head Charles to the Founder and Facilitator of "True Connections" Responsible Adults for Tomorrow.

Now let me drop this one hard on you. The umbilical cord that was connecting me to the madness of addiction has been cut off, and that unrighteous flow of self-destructive thinking and behavior can kiss my natural ass! Forgive me, Lord; I get caught up in the moment sometime (a lot of times, for real!). But do you feel what the brother saying?

What's the verdict? Will you take another ride with me? It's under construction, I call it "The Main Ingredients: The 10 Connections."

On a Personal Note: Recognitions of GRATITUDE

Gratitude to Individuals

- To Laurie Asplund, a licensed professional counselor, and author of "Justice Before Mercy." She showed up in my Queen's life, and her professional guidance was truly amazing from my perspective. She demonstrated the ability to "effectively communicate" with my wife. Laurie Asplund is truly a remarkable woman.

- To Christopher Coleman—I call him "Storm"—and Wynetta Coleman (that's my "Nina"!). They brought some spice into my life, but it's all good because the love is spicy, too!

- To Journey Mental Health Facility, Kayla and Mike, both therapists at the facility (though Kayla has moved on). We achieved a "True Connection." I was "visible" for real; they provided a demonstration of genuine concern.

Gratitude to the Counseling Staff at Elmhurst Home's treatment facility in Detroit.

I underwent two or three treatment experiences at the Elmhurt facility in either 2003 or 2004 (to tell you the truth, I don't remember). What I do know is that it was a Cognitive Behavioral Therapy Approach, and the counselors were tough, dressed real sharp, and were some pretty smart fellas for real!

They came across to me like they had a true command of their skills; they used the text books occasionally, but most of the time they shot straight from the hip! They were aggressive but not disrespectful; it was a true-to-life communication from counselor to client. This is where I witnessed up close and personal that butt-naked, in-the-raw, true-to-life approach from the "madness of addiction."

I didn't stay in treatment long enough to get the full benefit of what they had to offer, but check out what I did get. They talked about things from the "client's perspective," their personal madness. And they explained that the "awakening of the productive individual" was a process that had to be "Wanted and Sought After."

They taught that whatever we learned from the books, from each other, and from the counselors was to be experienced with an understanding that "any constructive thinking and behavioral change" would take place from deep down within, that it was time to take a serious and closer look at all of our insane behavior.

One counselor wrote on the chalkboard "Cognitive Restructuring," and told us to scrutinize the word "addiction." Had I been ready, I sincerely believe that this approach would have worked for me, but "just getting started" was more than difficult' it was not yet part of my plan. I was still tripping about my mama, my wife, and my brother-in-law's nonsense.

I left Elmhurst Home and went back in the madness. Thinking back on it now, I realize that the counselors in Detroit touched my mind, my heart, and my spirit in such a way! I took that Detroit flavor with me to Madison, WI, for real!

Gratitude to the Counseling Staff at Hope Haven's treatment setting in Madison, WI, 2006

- Kate Ihus, my supervisor, my mentor when I was the Resident Manager of Colvin Manor in 2007, and when I became a Substance Abuse Counselor in

Training. She gave the brother an opportunity to express himself through song, dance, skits, plays, and improvisations. It's hard to express my gratitude in words, I just know that she is an awesome Supervisor, a truly caring, wonderful human being!

- James Crawford, the Program Director when I was a client at the facility. He gave it up in the raw just like the counselors in Detroit. I'll never forget what he told me—check him out. "This life-changing experience is not for those who think it's a badge of honor to be locked down in the penitentiary!" He is now the CEO and Founder of Jessie Crawford Recovery Center in Madison, providing sober-living housing for individuals who truly want to experience the "Awakening of the Productive Individual."

- Barbra Purchase, a counselor at the facility, as well as my teacher when I became a Substance Abuse Counselor in Training. Her skill set at counseling manifested itself in her ability to do all the necessary paperwork (shift reports, treatment plans, after-care plans, etc.). She is awesome for real!

- Tamara, my counselor when I was a client at the facility. She gave it up in the raw as well—check her out. After I gave her my spiel about my life, she turned from her computer and spoke these words to me: "Get over yourself. You don't have a monopoly on pain, and this is not about drugs; this is about you. Now take your folder, and go to your room. You got two assignments, 'Unmanageability and Self Persecution.' Write about them and give it to me." She was out-cold, but that's just what the brother needed!

- Sarah and Nicole, the first staff personnel that I saw during intake. I don't remember which one of them told me "No" when I asked if I could stay there for a year. They were professional about it and came across with a genuine concern for me. I am truly grateful. (By the way, I stayed at Hope Haven for *two* years.)

- Mary Anne, so gracious, professional—she kept the office running smooth for real! She was a sweetheart, let me tell you!

- Don Mason, one of the counselors at the facility. He was a pretty sharp dresser, but he was sharp in mind as well and established a "connection" with the clients that prompted a "true engagement from counselor to client." He was a little animated (like me) and most effective.

- Rick Ness, another counselor at the facility. He assisted me with developing the proper attitude towards the clients and told me to maintain a healthy balance between my work and personal life.

- Freddy Clark, in charge of the internal workings of the facility (vendors, financial concerns, etc.). Freddy Clark is my buddy for real!

- Dave, the Chef at the facility, a very talented individual, gifted on so many levels. We had a "true connection."

- Valarie, the Kitchen Manager. When I started R.A.F.T., Responsible Adults for Tomorrow (a Men and Women's Empowerment Group), she assisted me on so many occasions with coffee, food, snacks and transportation for special presentations. I am truly grateful.

- Bruce Nichols, the head honcho at the facility. We didn't see eye to eye on the addiction/recovery process, but that's okay; he had the "Proper Hook

Up" as far as counselors go, let me be the first to tell you!

Acknowledgments

- Erving Goffman's *The Presentation of Self in Everyday Life* is a 1956 sociological book, in which the author uses the imagery of theater to portray the importance of human social interaction.

- Stanton Peele, Archie Brodsky, and Mary Arnold, *The Truth about Addiction and Recovery*.

- David J. Powell, *Clinical Supervision in Alcohol and Drug Abuse Counseling*.

- William L. White, *Slaying the Dragon: A History of Addiction Treatment and Recovery in America*.

- Vince Fox, *Addiction: Change and Choice*.

- Herbert Fingarette, *The Myth of Alcoholism as a Disease*.

- Charles Bufe, *Alcoholics Anonymous: Cult or Cure?*

- Pat Denning and Jeannie Little, *Over the Influence: The Harm-Reduction Guide to Controlling Your Drug and Alcohol Use*.

- Tina B. Tessina, *The Real Thirteenth Step*.

- Charlotte Davis Kasl, *Many Roads, One Journey: Moving Beyond the 12 Steps*.

- Bruce Alexander, *The Globalization of Addiction: A Study in Poverty of the Spirit*.

- Albert Ellis, *Overcoming Destructive Beliefs, Feelings, and Behavior*.

- Nathaniel Branden, *The Six Pillars of Self-Esteem*, *Taking Responsibility*, and *The Art of Living Consciously*.

- Jeffery Schaler, *Addiction is a Choice*.

- Marc Lewis, *The Biology of Desire: Why Addiction is not a Disease.*

- Eric Fromm, *Escape from Freedom*, *The Sane Society*, and *The Art of Loving.*

- B.F. Skinner, *About Behaviorism* and *Beyond Freedom and Dignity.*

- Carl G. Jung, *The Undiscovered Self* and *Carl Jung and Alcoholics Anonymous.*

- Zena Sharp and William S. Gray, who wrote to teach children how to read (*Fun with Dick and Jane, See Spot Run*).

- Jacob Grimm and Wilhelm Grimm, *Grimm Fairy Tales*, 1812-1858.

- Mark Twain, *The Adventures of Huckleberry Finn.*

- Charles Dickens, *Great Expectations.*

- *Sidney Poitier Meets Plato.* A 1964 album recorded by Warner Bros. Music, composed by Fred Katz.

Cognitive Behavioral Therapy was pioneered by Aaron T. Beck in the 1960s while he was a psychiatrist at the University of Pennsylvania. It is commonly defined as talk therapy—psychotherapy that can help with many emotional and mental conditions or issues. It is used by a host of professionals, therapists, counselors, etc. Albert Ellis formed a technique called the "ABC Technique of Irrational Beliefs," with an increased awareness of "damaging internal beliefs," with Cognitive Behavioral Therapy as a means to overcome destructive thinking and behavior.

Support Groups:

- Alcoholics Anonymous, founded in 1935 by Bill Wilson and Bob Smith. AA is a non-professional group, self-supporting and apolitical. Its only requirement for membership is a desire to stop drinking.

- Narcotics Anonymous, founded by Jimmy Kinnon in 1953. Narcotics Anonymous uses the 12-Step model that has been explained and developed for people with various substance-abuse issues. It is the second-largest 12-Step organization.

- Smart Recovery, founded by Joe Gerstein in 1994. Smart stands for "Self-Management and Recovery Training." Its approach uses cognitive-behavioral and non-confrontational motivational methods.

Honorable Mentions:

- Sly and the Family Stone, the lyrical genius of "It's a Family Affair" in 1971.

- My Dudes, my brothers from another mother, Daryl McCurty and Lawrence McCurty, for real! I sincerely believe that my Father who art in heaven placed these two awesome individuals in my life.

- Terry/Patricia Crawford, my brother, my sister, for real; let me be the first to tell you!

- Robin, a tower of strength for the brother when I was a client at Hope Haven. She moved on from client to counselor. You go, girl!

- D-Wayne Golden, my buddy for real; believe that!

- Edwina Meads—just like the brother, she went from client to counselor. This woman of God is my buddy for real!

- Trish, a presence with a command performance that's drenched in reality. She also moved on from client to counselor. She's a pistol for sho'!

- My Young Lion, C-Smooth the Music Man. I got that "Make it Make Sense" from him and ran with it!

- Carl, the brother responsible for my R.A.F.T. logo. I asked him to make it look like it came from God; he succeeded for real!

- My Queen—her name is Jennifer. A reconnection with Family. I now know why her Great Spirit and my Father in heaven put us together: for me to experience the "spontaneous free spirit" that permeates her soul; for me to grasp with a level of clarity, what's it like to be "her" (because she can be a pistol for real!); for her to experience a man that "truly loves her." I asked my Queen, "Can we grow old together?" and she said, "Yes" *Woo-wee!*

- To all my Family in Madison, the Love is Constant, the Love is Sure.

Closed for Repairs

Letters, Awards, & Recommendations

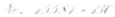

State of Wisconsin

Department of Regulation and Licensing

Hereby certifies that

CHARLES FOWLKES

was granted a license to practice as a

SUBSTANCE ABUSE COUNSELOR-IN-TRAINING

in the State of Wisconsin in accordance with Wisconsin law

on the 28th day of May, 2008

The authority granted herein must be renewed each biennium by the granting authority.

In witness thereof, the State of Wisconsin
Department of Regulation and Licensing

has caused this certificate to be issued under
the seal of the Department of Regulation and Licensing

Secretary

This license issued this 28th day of May, 2008

THE UNIVERSITY
of
WISCONSIN
MADISON

May 22, 2008

Mr. Charles Fowlkes
Hope Haven/ Rebos United
425 W. Johnson St.
Madison, WI 53703

Re: Substance Abuse & Mental Health lecture

Dear Mr. Fowlkes:

This letter is to express our gratitude for being a guest speaker in N105. Your presentation was dynamic and influential. One student pursued treatment for her addiction to marijuana that very same evening! As you will see in the comments below, your presentation opened the doors for other students to consider making positive life changing decisions. Your presentation was in the top three most valued lectures according to the students. Here are just a few of the written comments from the students:

"Charles' presentation gives me hope. So much about substance abuse can really get you depressed. He's actually been through treatment and now is a success story. I've never talked to someone who's been through treatment before."

"According to his [Mr. Doram's] definition, I am a binge drinker and so are my roommates. I would never have thought about it until today. I need to talk to them [roommates] about it."

"You could tell that they both [Mr. Fowlkes and Mr. Doram] knew what they were talking about!"

"In the medical fields, we will always have to deal with substance abuse and watch for it. Addiction is a disease and no matter where you work, you must be ready to handle these issues."

"Charles was great! Going from crack head to everything better was an inspiration! I'm going to remember what he said for a long time—'I'm a soldier under construction for the rest of my life.'"

"I guess my roommate has a problem with drinking because it's interfering with school. He's been out drinking instead of studying and he's missed a lot of classes."

"You hear a lot about drug abuse these days, but not much on alcohol. I'd like to hear more about alcohol addiction. I think alcohol is more dangerous because you can get it anywhere."

"I think it is very important that both mental health professionals and substance abuse professionals learn more about each other's fields in order to more efficiently and accurately diagnose, co-diagnose and treat patients."

Your personal story along with Mr. Doram's presentation was very successful in communicating your message to the students. We appreciate your expertise and easy connection with the students.

Sincerely,

Sarah Kruger, R.N., M.S., APNP
Clinical Associate Professor
600 Highland Ave CSC H6/266
Madison, WI 53792-2455
Email: stkruger@wisc.edu

Elizabeth Batz, R.N., M.S., APNP
Teaching Assistant
600 Highland Ave. CSC K6/117
Madison, WI 53792-2455
Email: embatz@wisc.edu

School of Nursing
University of Wisconsin-Madison   600 Highland Avenue   Madison, Wisconsin 53792-2455
http://www.son.wisc.edu/

HOPE HAVEN·REBOS
UNITED

HOPE HAVEN
425 W. JOHNSON ST.
MADISON. WI 53703
(608) 255-0359

Minority Counselor Training Institute
Wisconsin Association on Alcohol & Other
Drug Abuse
6601 Grand Teton Plaza, Suite A
Madison, WI 53719

08-27-07

To Whom It May Concern:

I am writing this letter as a recommendation that the Minority Training Institute accept Charles Fowlkes as a candidate for entrance into the program. I have known Mr. Fowlkes for over a year and can attest to the passion with which he lives his personal recovery program and the dedication that he has to helping others with their journey. He currently functions as the Resident Manager for Colvin Manor, a ¾ house that is operated under my direct supervision. The Resident Manager is a peer lead position responsible for overseeing that the residence is kept clean, drug free, and safe from violence and/or other potential problems. It is also his job to keep Hope Haven Staff informed of any and all concerns related to any observations he may have regarding either Hope Haven or Colvin Manor residents. Mr. Fowlkes also conducts bi-monthly House Meetings and collects rent from the residents.

Mr. Fowlkes has consistently demonstrated his ability to relate to and communicate effectively with the residents. He is considered approachable, honest, and fair, by his peers, and is well respected by both the residents and the staff. Mr. Fowlkes is a very hard worker and has been willing to take on additional responsibilities as they have been brought to him. He is also very quick to find ways to improve on the process and procedures that make the residence a better running facility.

Mr. Fowlkes is dedicated to advancing his knowledge and his role as a counselor for individuals seeking assistance from addictions. He has not only shown leadership by assuming the role of Resident Manager but he has creatively developed and implemented a support group called R.A.F.T. (Responsible Adults For Tomorrow). R.A.F.T. is an innovative approach to assisting individuals with their recovery process. It is another unique support group offered on a continuum of support groups and many Hope Haven and Colvin Manor residents have found the group to be very important in their recovery process.

It is my considered opinion that the Minority Counselor Training Institute would be proud to have such a fine individual among your ranks of successful graduates, therefore, I would encourage you to grant him entrance to your program. If you would like additional information in support of Mr. Fowlkes, please do not hesitate to contact me. I would be most happy to provide you with any thing to make your selection process of Mr. Fowlkes successful.

Sincerely,

Kate Ihus, LPC, SAC, ICS
Associate Director
Hope Haven Rebos United
(608) 772-1133

www.ingramcontent.com/pod-product-compliance
Lightning Source LLC
Chambersburg PA
CBHW060351130626
46553CB00003B/1174